Mountaintop Mornings
for
Forty Days

To my Mom who wanted a
devotional for her purse.
Love you so much!

INTRODUCTION

The power in prayer is found in God's Word, not
our voice; it's God's voice, not our words.

God's word is timeless. It meets every need. It is
the power of the Holy Spirit moving and
breathing here on earth in the lives of God's
children. God's word is an invitation to everyone
to enter into a sweet relationship with Himself.
He wants to speak to you. He wants you to hear
His voice speak into your specific situation as you
cry out to Him. When you pray God's word,
mountains move effortlessly. Your heart is
aligning with God's heart in a perfect position to
battle.

So often, we believe we have to physically get
away to a mountain to be refreshed, recharged, or
renewed to tackle what God has placed before us.
We want to meet with God. We want God to meet
with us. We need His presence. We need His
voice so clear. Yes, God meets people on the
mountain when they physically step away to seek
Him. Yes, when people get away from the
distractions in daily life they hear God. However,
not everyone can physically depart from the
everyday for a retreat; and yet we all can have a

mountaintop experience every morning when we read God's word, seeking to hear His clear voice. God wants to talk to you every day. He wants to hear your voice every day. He desires a dialogue, not a monologue. When you talk to God and read His Word, you enter into a conversation that transforms your heart—**Romans 12:1-2,** and gives you peace of mind—**Philippians 4:6-7**. And then when you begin praying His word, you show your submission to His Sovereign plan. God is all knowing. He knows what is best for every situation. Trust Him!

Mountaintop Mornings for Forty Days is a devotional that fits in a purse or pocket and is pure scripture. Every devotion ends with an "Amen," as each devotion is a prayer; praying through scripture. It is my prayer that as you pray through scripture you will hear God speak directly to your heart. Whatever is concerning you right now, God has a word for you. He wants to comfort you, encourage you, and exhort you to right living. He loves you so much! It is also my prayer that we would be a generation that seeks to hear God's voice over man's voice. Who doesn't love a good word found in a prayer journal? There are a lot of wise people that seem to spout gold all day long. However, the BEST journal is God's journal — the story of redemption proclaimed in the Bible. God redeeming mankind from the destructiveness of sin through Jesus Christ's death and resurrection. He says it the BEST! All wisdom comes from God's word; it "is a tree of life to those who take hold of her, and happy are all who retain her" — **Proverbs 3:18 NKJV**. The wisdom you need, God has supplied. You simply need to seek Him — **Jeremiah 29:13**, and ask — **James 1:5**.

God bless you!
:: *Alysa VanderWeerd*

READER'S GUIDE

There are many ways you can utilize this devotional as a tool to grow closer to God. The goal of every Christian is to know God — to know God's heart, to live His heart, and to share His heart with others. His heart is His word.

1. You can pray the Scripture verses each day.

"Because of Christ and our faith in Him, we can now come fearlessly into God's presence assured of His glad welcome." — **Ephesians 3:12 NLT**

Every day you can enter God's presence knowing He wants to hear from you. He absolutely loves you and He loves those you care about. You don't have to fear. Jesus Christ's death on the cross forgave the sin that separated you from God. He rose again and is now seated at God's right hand; Jesus is praying for you specifically. He lives to intercede for you — **Hebrews 7:25**.

When you pray God's word, you are aligning your heart with His heart for whom you are praying; saying, "Not my will Lord, but Yours be done" — **Luke 22:42**.

You can pray the verses for:

> Your church
> Family
> Friends
> Yourself
> Nation
> Spiritual Leaders
> Workplace
> Co-workers
> School
> Community Group
> Or anyone else God places on your heart

2. You can study each verse provided for on the given day.

   a.) Pray and ask God by the power of His Holy Spirit to illuminate His truth to you.

"All Scripture is inspired by God and is useful to teach us what is true and to make us realize what is wrong in our lives. It straightens us out and teaches us to do what is right. It is God's way of preparing us in every way, fully equipped for every good thing God wants us to do."
Timothy 3:16-17 NLT

b.) Take one verse at a time.
- o What is the main concept of the verse?
- o What is God speaking to you personally?
- o How can you apply that verse to your life? How can you live this word?
- o Who does God want you to share this word with?

c.) As you read all of the verses, ask how they connect with each other?
- o Do some verses provide a greater depth of meaning to the first verse?
- o Is there a consistent theme in all of the verses?
- o What is the overall take away truth?
- o How can you live this truth?
- o Who can you share this truth with?

3. A journal is provided within the pages.

At a glance, you will be able to see what God has spoken to your heart. It is healthy to look back at your steps in history to see what choices brought you to today. Remembering those moments God called you to obey, ignites your heart with passion; while, recalling His deliverances affirms your faith.

God loves you so much! Every day matters. Your decisions today affect your tomorrows; they affect your family and all those around you. So, when you sit before the Lord, it is always good to ask Him to search your heart; to point out anything within you that offends Him — **Psalm 139:23-24**. Our thoughts affect our emotions, which in turn affect our actions. God is so faithful to correct our wrong thinking by directing us to His Word and right thinking. We then repent of sin and leave transformed, submitted to His Word — **Romans 12:1-2**.

But so too, the Lord comforts the afflicted and encourages the downcast with a right word at the right time. He strengthens us when we are tempted — **Hebrews 2:18**; He corrects us with right discipline — **Hebrews 12:5**; He provides for all our needs — **Philippians 4:19**; He keeps every promise — **Romans 4:20**. God is faithful — **2 Timothy 2:13**!

Life is purifying. We are all in the Refiner's fire, going from glory to greater glory — **2 Corinthians 3:18**. But there is One who stands with us in the flame, never leaving us alone. With our eyes on Jesus
Christ, the Great Shepherd of the sheep, we can endure until the end.

Patient endurance is what you need right now so that you are able to continue to do God's will — **Hebrews 10:36**. He is with you. He knows you. He loves you!

Do you desire to know Him on a deeper level?

In this life, learning never ends; every day it sharpens your mind, preparing you to see Jesus Christ face to face.

DAY 1

This Book of the Law shall not depart from your mouth, but you shall meditate in it day and night, that you may observe to do according to all that is written in it. For then you will make your way prosperous, and then you will have good success. * Blessed is the man who walks not in the counsel of the ungodly, nor stands in the path of sinners, nor sits in the seat of the scornful; but his delight is in the law of the LORD, and in His law he meditates day and night. He shall be like a tree planted by the rivers of water, that brings forth it's fruit in its season, whose leaf also shall not wither; and whatever he does shall prosper. * No good thing will He withhold from those who walk uprightly. * Blessed are the undefiled in the way, who walk in the law of the LORD! * And blessed be His glorious name forever! And let the whole earth be filled with His glory. Amen and Amen.

Joshua 1:8 NKJV * Psalm 1:1-3 NKJV * Psalm 84:11 NKJV * Psalm 119:1 NKJV * Psalm 72:19 NKJV

DAY

1 ....

Why is God's Word important?

_____

_____

_____

_____

_____

_____

_____

_____

_____

_____

_____

_____

_____

_____

_____

_____

_____

_____

_____

_____

_____

DAY 2

If we say that we have no sin, we deceive ourselves, and the truth is not in us. * What fruit did you have then in the things which you are now ashamed? For the end of those things is death. * For the wages of sin is death, but the gift of God is eternal life in Christ Jesus our Lord. * For I acknowledge my transgressions, and my sin is always before me. Against You, You only, have I sinned, and done this evil in Your sight—that You may be found just when You speak, and blameless when You judge. * I don't understand myself at all, for I really want to do what is right, but I don't do it. Instead I do the very thing I hate. I know perfectly well that what I am doing is wrong, and my bad conscience shows that I agree that the law is good. But I can't help myself, because it is sin inside of me that makes me do these evil things. * When I want to do good, I don't. And when I try not to do wrong, I do it anyway. * If we confess our sins, He is faithful and just to forgive us our sins and to cleanse us from all unrighteousness. * For He made Him who knew no sin to be sin for us, that we might become the righteousness of God in Him. * Create in me a clean heart, O God and renew a steadfast spirit within me. Do not cast me away from Your presence, and do not take Your Holy Spirit from me. Restore to me the joy of Your salvation, and uphold me by Your generous Spirit. * Amen and Amen.

1 John 1:8 NKJV * Romans 6:21 NKJV * Romans 6:23 NKJV * Psalm 51:3-4 NKJV * Romans 7:15-17 NLT * Romans 7:19 NLT * 1 John 1:9 NKJV * 2 Corinthians 5:21 NKJV * Psalm 51:10-12 NKJV * Psalm 72:19b NKJV

DAY

2 . . . .

Against God, you have sinned.

_____

_____

_____

_____

_____

_____

_____

_____

_____

_____

_____

_____

_____

_____

_____

_____

_____

_____

_____

_____

DAY 3

For we are His workmanship, created in Christ
Jesus for good works, which God prepared
beforehand that we should walk in them. * Every
good gift and every perfect gift is from above, and
comes down from the Father of lights, with whom
is no variation or shadow of turning. * If any of
you lacks wisdom, let him ask of God, who gives
to all liberally and without reproach, and it will
be given to him. * Then the word of
the LORD came to me, saying: "Before I formed
you in the womb I knew you; before you were
born I sanctified you; I ordained you a prophet to
the nations." Then said I: "Ah, Lord GOD! Behold,
I cannot speak, for I am a youth." But the LORD
said to me: "Do not say, 'I am a youth,' for you
shall go to all to whom I send you, and whatever I
command you, you shall speak. Do not be afraid
of their faces, for I am with you to deliver you,"
says the LORD. * Amen and Amen.

Ephesians 2:10 NKJV * James 1:17 NKJV * James
1:5 NKJV * Jeremiah 1:4-8 NKJV * Psalm 72:19b
NKJV

3 ....

You are God's workmanship, created with a calling.

_____

_____

_____

_____

_____

_____

_____

_____

_____

_____

_____

_____

_____

_____

_____

_____

_____

_____

_____

_____

DAY 4

No eye has seen, no ear has heard, and no mind has imagined what God has prepared for those who love him. * For with God nothing will be impossible. * Walk in wisdom toward those who are outside, redeeming the time. Let your speech always be with grace, seasoned with salt, that you may know how you ought to answer each one. * Let the word of Christ dwell in you richly in all wisdom, teaching and admonishing one another in psalms and hymns and spiritual songs, singing with grace in your hearts to the Lord. And whatever you do in word or deed, do all in the name of the Lord Jesus, giving thanks to God the Father through Him. * Your obedience has become known to all. * Therefore, whether you eat or drink or whatever you do, do all to the glory of God. * And whatever you do, do it heartily, as to the Lord and not to men, knowing that from the Lord you will receive the reward of the inheritance for you serve the Lord Christ. * For I am not ashamed of the gospel of Christ, for it is the power of God to salvation for everyone who believes, for the Jew first and also for the Greek. * And the God of peace will crush Satan under your feet shortly. The grace of our Lord Jesus Christ be with you. Amen.

1 Corinthians 2:9 NLT * Luke 1:37 NKJV *
Colossians 3:16-17 NKJV * Romans 16:19a NKJV *
1 Corinthians 10:31 NKJV * Colossians 4:5-6 NKJV
* Colossians 3:23 NKJV * Romans 1:16 NKJV *
Romans 16:20 NKJV

4 ....

God has great plans for you.

_____

_____

_____

_____

_____

_____

_____

_____

_____

_____

_____

_____

_____

_____

_____

_____

_____

_____

_____

DAY 5

There is a time for everything, and a season for every activity under the heavens. * A time to be born and a time to die, a time to plant and a time to uproot. * A time to kill and a time to heal, a time to tear down and a time to build. * A time to weep and a time to laugh, a time to mourn and a time to dance. * A time to scatter stones and a time to gather them, a time to embrace and a time to refrain from embracing. * A time to search and a time to give up, a time to keep and a time to throw away. * A time to tear and a time to mend, a time to be silent and a time to speak. * A time to love and a time to hate, a time for war and a time for peace. * He has made everything beautiful in its time. He has also set eternity in the human heart; yet no one can fathom what God has done from beginning to end. * To the only wise God be glory forever through Jesus Christ! Amen.

Ecclesiastes 3:1 NIV * Ecclesiastes 3:2 NIV * Ecclesiastes 3:3 NIV * Ecclesiastes 3:4 NIV * Ecclesiastes 3:5 NIV * Ecclesiastes 3:6 NIV * Ecclesiastes 3:7 NIV * Ecclesiastes 3:8 NIV * Ecclesiastes 3:11 NIV * Romans 16:27 NIV

DAY

5 ....

It is the time to ...

_____

_____

_____

_____

_____

_____

_____

_____

_____

_____

_____

_____

_____

_____

_____

_____

_____

_____

_____

_____

DAY 6

But You are the same, and Your years will have
no end. * "I am the Alpha and the Omega, the
Beginning and the End," says the Lord, "who is
and who was and who is to come, the Almighty."
* "For I am the LORD, I do not change." * Oh, give
thanks to the LORD, for He is good! For His mercy
endures forever. * For I am persuaded that neither
death nor life, nor angels nor principalities nor
powers, nor things present nor things to come,
nor height nor depth, nor any other created thing,
shall be able to separate us from the love of God
which is in Christ Jesus our Lord. * Jesus Christ is
the same yesterday, today, and forever. * Amen
and Amen.

Psalm 102:27 NKJV * Revelation 1:8 NKJV *
Malachi 3:6a NKJV * Psalm 136:1 NKJV * Romans
8:38-39 NKJV * Hebrews 13:8 NKJV * Psalm
41:13b NKJV

DAY

6 ....

The Beginning and the End will never change.

_____

_____

_____

_____

_____

_____

_____

_____

_____

_____

_____

_____

_____

_____

_____

_____

_____

_____

DAY 7

I love your sanctuary, LORD, the place where your glory shines. * My heart has heard you say, "Come and talk with me." And my heart responds, "LORD, I am coming." * My life is an example to many, because you have been my strength and protection. That is why I can never stop praising you; I declare your glory all day long. * The LORD is my shepherd; I have everything I need. * Surely your goodness and unfailing love will pursue me all the days of my life, and I will live in the house of the LORD forever. * Bless his glorious name forever! Let the whole earth be filled with his glory. Amen and Amen!

Psalm 26:8 NLT * Psalm 27:8 NLT * Psalm 71:7-8 NLT * Psalm 23:1 NLT * Psalm 23:6 NLT * Psalm 72:19 NLT

DAY

7. ....

Is your life filled with self-efficacy or God dependency?

_____
_____
_____
_____
_____
_____
_____
_____
_____
_____
_____
_____
_____
_____
_____
_____
_____
_____
_____
_____
_____

DAY 8

He who dwells in the secret place of the Most High shall abide under the shadow of the Almighty. I will say of the LORD, "He is my refuge and my fortress; my God, in Him I will trust." * Trust in the LORD forever, for YAH, the LORD, is everlasting strength. For He brings down those who dwell on high, the lofty city; He lays it low, He lays it low to the ground, He brings it down to the dust. The foot shall tread it down — the feet of the poor and the steps of the needy. * Surely He shall deliver you from the snare of the fowler and from the perilous pestilence. He shall cover you with His feathers, and under His wings you shall take refuge; His truth shall be your shield and buckler. You shall not be afraid of the terror by night, nor of the arrow that flies by day. Nor of the pestilence that walks in darkness, nor of the destruction that lays waste at noonday. * Jesus said to him, "I am the way, the truth, and the life. No one comes to the Father except through Me." * Let not your heart be troubled; you believe in God, believe also in Me. * A thousand may fall at your side, and ten thousand at your right hand; but it shall not come near you. Only with your eyes shall you look, and see the reward of the wicked. Because you have made the LORD, who is my refuge, even the Most High, your dwelling place, no evil shall befall you, nor shall any plague come near your dwelling; for He shall give His angels charge over you, to keep you in all your ways. In their hands they shall bear you up, lest you dash your foot against a stone. * Open the gates, that the righteous nation which keeps truth may enter in. You will keep him in perfect peace, whose mind is stayed on You, because he trusts in You. * Because he has set his love upon Me, therefore I will deliver him; I will set him on high, because he has known My name. He shall call upon Me, and I will answer him; I will be with him in trouble; I will deliver him and honor him. With long life I will satisfy him, and show him My salvation. * Now to the King eternal, immortal, invisible, to God who alone is wise, be honor and glory forever and ever. Amen.

Psalm 91:1-2 NKJV * Isaiah 26:3-6 NKJV * Psalm 91:3-6 NKJV * John 14:6 NKJV * John 14:1 NKJV * Psalm 91:7-12 NKJV * Isaiah 26:2-3 NKJV * Psalm 91:14-16 NKJV * 1 Timothy 1:17 NKJV

DAY

8 . . . .

God's Presence protects.

_____

_____

_____

_____

_____

_____

_____

_____

_____

_____

_____

_____

_____

_____

_____

_____

_____

_____

_____

_____

_____

_____

_____

Here is my final conclusion: Fear God and obey his commands, for this is the duty of every person. God will judge us for everything we do, including every secret thing, whether good or bad. * But even though a person sins a hundred times and still lives a long time, I know that those who fear God will be better off. The wicked will never live long, good lives, for they do not fear God. Their days will never grow long like the evening shadows. * So try to walk a middle course — but those who fear God will succeed either way. * Fear of the LORD is the beginning of wisdom. Knowledge of the Holy One results in understanding. * Fear of the LORD is the beginning of knowledge. Only fools despise wisdom and discipline. * Reverence for the LORD is the foundation of true wisdom. The rewards of wisdom come to all who obey him. Praise his name forever! * Praise the LORD! Happy are those who fear the LORD. Yes, happy are those who delight in doing what he commands. * Bless his glorious name forever! Let the whole earth be filled with his glory. Amen and Amen.

Ecclesiastes 12:13-14 NLT * Ecclesiastes 8:12-13 NLT * Ecclesiastes 7:18 NLT * Proverbs 9:10 NLT *

Proverbs 1:7 NLT * Psalm 111:10 NLT * Psalm 112:1 NLT * Psalm 72:19 NLT

9 . . . .

Walking in the fear of the Lord is foundational.

_____

_____

_____

_____

_____

_____

_____

_____

_____

_____

_____

_____

_____

_____

_____

_____

_____

_____

_____

_____

_____

DAY 10

You are my hiding place and my shield; I hope in
Your word. * You are my hiding place; You shall
preserve me from trouble; You shall surround me
with songs of deliverance. * The angel of the
LORD encamps all around those who fear Him,
and delivers them. * For the arms of the wicked
shall be broken, but the LORD upholds the
righteous. * No evil shall befall you, nor shall any
plague come near your dwelling; for He shall give
His angels charge over you, to keep you in all
your ways. In their hands they shall bear you up,
lest you dash your foot against a stone. * Truly my
soul silently waits for God; from Him comes my
salvation. He only is my rock and my salvation;
He is my defense; I shall not be greatly moved. *
Trust in Him at all times, you people; pour out
your heart before Him; God is a refuge for us. *
Amen and Amen.

Psalm 119:114 NKJV * Psalm 32:7 NKJV * Psalm
34:7 NKJV * Psalm 37:17 NKJV * Psalm 62:1-2
NKJV * Psalm 91:10-12 NKJV * Psalm 72:19b
NKJV

DAY

10 ....

The perfect hiding place shields His own.

_____

_____

_____

_____

_____

_____

_____

_____

_____

_____

_____

_____

_____

_____

_____

_____

_____

_____

_____

_____

Come, bless the LORD, all you servants of the
LORD, who stand by night in the house of the
LORD! Lift up your hands to the holy place and
bless the LORD! * Bless the LORD, O my soul, and
all that is within me, bless his holy name! Bless
the LORD, O my soul, and forget not all his
benefits, who forgives all your iniquity, who heals
all your diseases, who redeems your life from the
pit, who crowns you with steadfast love and
mercy, who satisfies you with good so that your
youth is renewed like the eagle's. * I will extol
you, my God and King, and bless your name
forever and ever. Every day I will bless you and
praise your name forever and ever. * All your
works shall give thanks to you, O LORD, and all
your saints shall bless you! They shall speak of the
glory of your kingdom and tell of your power, to
make known to the children of man your mighty
deeds, and the glorious splendor of your
kingdom. * Amen and Amen!

Psalm 134:1-2 ESV * Psalm 103:1-5 ESV * Psalm
145:1-2 ESV * Psalm 145:10-12 ESV * Psalm 72:19b
ESV

DAY

11 . . . .

Bless the LORD, O my soul!

_____

_____

_____

_____

_____

_____

_____

_____

_____

_____

_____

_____

_____

_____

_____

_____

_____

_____

_____

_____

DAY 12

At midnight I will rise to give thanks to You, because of Your righteous judgments. * Your commands make me wiser than my enemies, for your commands are my constant guide. * Your word is a lamp to my feet and a light to my path. * I am afflicted very much; revive me according to Your word. * I have inclined my heart to perform Your statutes forever, to the very end. * The entrance of Your word gives light; it gives understanding to the simple. * Make Your face shine upon Your servant, and teach me Your statutes. * Your word is very pure; therefore Your servant loves it. * I rejoice at Your word as one who finds great treasure. * My lips shall utter praise, for You teach me Your statutes. * My tongue shall speak of Your word, for all Your commandments are righteousness. * I long for Your salvation, O LORD, and Your law is my delight. * Amen, and Amen.

Psalm 119:62 NKJV * Psalm 119:98 NLT * Psalm 119:105 NKJV * Psalm 119:107 NKJV * Psalm 119:112 NKJV * Psalm 119:130 NKJV * Psalm 119:135 NKJV * Psalm 119:140 NKJV * Psalm 119:162 NKJV * Psalm 119:171 NKJV * Psalm 119:172 NKJV * Psalm 119:174 NKJV * Psalm 72:19b KJV

DAY

12 ....

God teaches His words of truth.

_____

_____
_____
_____
_____
_____
_____
_____
_____
_____
_____
_____
_____
_____
_____
_____
_____
_____
_____
_____
_____
_____

DAY 13

Serve the LORD with gladness! Come into his presence with singing! * Praise the LORD! For it is good to sing praises to our God; for it is pleasant, and a song of praise is fitting. * Seek the LORD and his strength; seek his presence continually! * Enter his gates with thanksgiving, and his courts with praise! Give thanks to him; bless his name! * The eyes of the LORD are toward the righteous and his ears toward their cry. * I cry aloud to God, aloud to God, and he will hear me. * He heals the brokenhearted and binds up their wounds. * The LORD redeems the life of his servants; none of those who take refuge in him will be condemned. * You open your hand; you satisfy the desire of every living thing. * You make known to me the path of life; in your presence there is fullness of joy; at your right hand are pleasures forevermore. * I said, "Let me remember my song in the night; let me meditate in my heart." Then my spirit made a diligent search. * By day the LORD commands his steadfast love, and at night his song is with me, a prayer to the God of my life. * Blessed be his glorious name forever; may the whole earth be filled with his glory! Amen and Amen!

Psalm 100:2 ESV * Psalm 147:1 ESV * Psalm 105:4 ESV * Psalm 100:4 ESV * Psalm 34:15 ESV * Psalm 77:1 ESV * Psalm 147:3 ESV * Psalm 34:22 ESV * Psalm 145:16 ESV * Psalm 16:11 ESV * Psalm 77:6 ESV * Psalm 42:8 ESV * Psalm 72:19 ESV

DAY

13.....................................

God hears your voice.

_____
_____
_____
_____
_____
_____
_____
_____
_____
_____
_____
_____
_____
_____
_____
_____
_____
_____
_____
_____
_____
_____

Now when Sanballat, Tobiah, the Arabs, the Ammonites and the Ashdodites heard that the repair of the walls of Jerusalem went on, and that the breaches began to be closed, they were very angry. All of them conspired together to come and fight against Jerusalem and to cause a disturbance in it. But we prayed to our God, and because of them we set up a guard against them day and night. * Our enemies said, "They will not know or see until we come among them, kill them and put a stop to the work." * When I saw their fear, I rose and spoke to the nobles, the officials and the rest of the people: "Do not be afraid of them; remember the Lord who is great and awesome, and fight for your brothers, your sons, your daughters, your wives and your houses." When our enemies heard that it was known to us, and that God had frustrated their plan, then all of us returned to the wall, each one to his work. * So we carried on the work with half of them holding spears from dawn until the stars appeared. At that time I also said to the people, "Let each man with his servant spend the night within Jerusalem so that they may be a guard for us by night and a laborer by day." So neither I, my brothers, my servants, nor the men of the guard who followed me, none of us removed our clothes, each took his weapon even to the water. * Without wise leadership, a nation falls. * Amen, and Amen.

Nehemiah 4:7-9 NASB * Nehemiah 4:11 NASB * Nehemiah 4:14-15 NASB * Nehemiah 4:21-23 NASB * Proverbs 11:14a NLT * Psalm 72:19b NASB

DAY

14 ....

A nation rests under wise leadership.

_____
_____
_____
_____
_____
_____
_____
_____
_____
_____
_____
_____
_____
_____
_____
_____
_____
_____
_____
_____
_____
_____

DAY 15

I will give thanks to You, for I am fearfully and wonderfully made; wonderful are Your works, and my soul knows it very well. * Your eyes have seen my unformed substance; and in Your book were all written the days that were ordained for me, when as yet there was not one of them. * For we are His workmanship, created in Christ Jesus for good works, which God prepared beforehand so that we would walk in them. * That is what the Scriptures mean when they say, "No eye has seen, no ear has heard, and no mind has imagined what God has prepared for those who love him." * For I know the thoughts that I think toward you, says the Lord, thoughts of peace and not of evil, to give you a future and a hope. * Now the God of peace, who brought up from the dead the great Shepherd of the sheep through the blood of the eternal covenant, even Jesus our Lord, equip you in every good thing to do His will, working in us that which is pleasing in His sight, through Jesus Christ, to whom be the glory forever and ever. Amen.

Psalm 139:14 NASB * Psalm 139:16 NASB * Ephesians 2:10 NASB * 1 Corinthians 2:9 NLT * Jeremiah 29:11 NKJV * Hebrews 13:20-21 NASB

DAY

15 . . . .

God's thoughts about you are full of peace.

_____
_____
_____
_____
_____
_____
_____
_____
_____
_____
_____
_____
_____
_____
_____
_____
_____
_____
_____
_____
_____
_____

Every word of God is pure; He is a shield to those who put their trust in Him. * Your word is very pure; therefore Your servant loves it. * For You, O LORD, will bless the righteous; with favor You will surround him as with a shield. * As for God, His way is perfect; the word of the LORD is proven; He is a shield to all who trust in Him. * You also have given me the shield of your salvation; Your right hand has held me up, Your gentleness has made me great. * You, O LORD, are a shield for me, my glory and the One who lifts up my head. * Truly my soul silently waits for God; from Him comes my salvation. He only is my rock and my salvation; He is my defense; I shall not be greatly moved. * As for me, You uphold me in my integrity, and set me before Your face forever. Blessed be the LORD God of Israel from everlasting to everlasting! Amen and Amen.

Proverbs 30:5 NKJV * Psalm 119:140 NKJV * Psalm 5:12 NKJV * Psalm 18:30 NKJV * Psalm 18:35 NKJV * Psalm 3:3 NKJV * Psalm 62:1-2 NKJV * Psalm 41:12-13 NKJV

16 ....

The Word of God is your purest defense.

_____
_____
_____
_____
_____
_____
_____
_____
_____
_____
_____
_____
_____
_____
_____
_____
_____
_____
_____
_____
_____
_____

Therefore be patient, brethren, until the coming of the Lord. See how the farmer waits for the precious fruit of the earth, wait patiently for it until it receives the early or latter rain. You also be patient. Establish your hearts, for the coming of the Lord is at hand. * The Lord isn't really being slow about his promise to return, as some people think. No, he is being patient for your sake. He does not want anyone to perish, so he is giving more time for everyone to repent. * And so, dear friends, while you are waiting for these things to happen, make every effort to live a pure and blameless life. And be at peace with God. * In this you greatly rejoice, though now for a little while, if need be, you have been grieved by various trials, that the genuineness of your faith, being more precious than gold that perishes, though it is tested by fire, may be found to praise, honor, and glory at the revelation of Jesus Christ, whom having not seen you love. Though now you do not see Him, yet believing, you rejoice with joy inexpressible and full of glory, receiving the end of your faith — the salvation of your souls. * So think clearly and exercise self-control. Look forward to the special blessings that will come to you at the return of Jesus Christ. * We are bound to give thanks to God always for you, brethren beloved by the Lord, because God from the beginning chose you for salvation through sanctification by the Spirit and belief in the truth, to which He called you by our gospel, for the obtaining of the glory of our Lord Jesus Christ. * He who is the faithful witness to all these things says, "Yes, I am coming soon!" Amen! Come, Lord Jesus!

James 5:7-8 NKJV * 2 Peter 3:9 NLT * 2 Peter 3:14 NLT * 1 Peter 1:6-9 NKJV * 1 Peter 1:13 NLT * 2 Thessalonians 2:13-14 NKJV * Revelation 22:20 NLT

17 . . . .

Fruit is born as you patiently wait.

_____
_____
_____
_____
_____
_____
_____
_____
_____
_____
_____
_____
_____
_____
_____
_____
_____
_____
_____
_____
_____

DAY 18

Thus says the LORD, the King of Israel, and his Redeemer, the LORD of hosts: I am the First and I am the Last; besides Me there is no God. * Most assuredly, I say to you, before Abraham was, I AM. * Fear not, for I am with you; be not dismayed, for I am your God; I will strengthen you, I will help you, I will uphold you with my righteous right hand. * For I am the LORD, I do not change. * I am the light of the world. He who follows Me shall not walk in darkness, but have the light of life. * In Him was life, and the life was the light of men. * I am the bread of life. He who comes to Me shall never hunger, and he who believes in Me shall never thirst. * I am from above. * I am not of this world. * I am the door. If anyone enters by Me, he will be saved, and will go in and out and find pasture. * I am the good shepherd. The good shepherd gives His life for the sheep. * I am the resurrection and the life. He who believes in Me, though he may die, he shall live. * I am the way, the truth and the life. No one comes to the Father except through Me. * "I am the Alpha and the Omega, the Beginning and the End," says the Lord, "who is and who was and who is to come, the Almighty." * Do not be afraid; I am the First and the Last. I am He who lives, and was dead, and behold, I am alive forevermore. Amen.

Isaiah 44:6 NKJV * John 8:58 NKJV * Isaiah 41:10 NKJV * Malachi 3:6 NKJV * * John 8:12b NKJV * John 1:4 NKJV * John 6:35 NKJV * John 8:23a NKJV * John 8:23b NKJV * John 10:9 NKJV * John 10:11 NKJV * John 11:25 NKJV * John 14:6 NKJV * Revelation 1:8 NKJV * Revelation 1:17b NKJV

18. . . . .

The Great I AM provides for you in every way.

_____

_____

_____

_____

_____

_____

_____

_____

_____

_____

_____

_____

_____

_____

_____

_____

_____

_____

_____

_____

_____

DAY 19

But earnestly desire the best gifts. And yet I show you a more excellent way. * The greatest of these is love. * Greater love has no one than this, than to lay down one's life for his friends. * Beloved, let us love one another, for love is of God; and everyone who loves is born of God and knows God. He who does not love does not know God, for God is love. In this the love of God was manifested toward us, that God has sent His only begotten Son into the world, that we might live through Him. * We love Him because He first loved us. * Therefore, be imitators of God as dear children. And walk in love, as Christ also has loved us and given Himself for us, an offering and a sacrifice to God for a sweet-smelling aroma. * We know how much God loves us, and we have put our trust in Him. God is love, and all who live in love live in God, and God lives in them. And as we live in God, our love grows more perfect. So we will not be afraid on the day of judgment, but can face him with confidence because we are like Christ here in this world. * Love is patient and kind. Love is not jealous or boastful or proud or rude. Love does not demand its own way. Love is not irritable, and it keeps no record of when it has been wronged. It is never glad about injustice but rejoices whenever the truth wins out. Love never gives up, never loses faith, is always hopeful, and endures through every circumstance. Love will last forever. * My little children, let us not love in word or in tongue, but in deed and truth. * There is no fear in love; but perfect love casts out fear, because fear involves torment. But he who fears has not been made perfect in love. * Little children, keep yourselves from idols. Amen.

1 Corinthians 12:31 NKJV * 1 Corinthians 13:13 NKJV * John 15:13 NKJV * 1 John 4:7-9 NKJV * 1 John 4:19 NKJV * Ephesians 5:1-2 NKJV * 1 John 4:16-17 NLT * 1 Corinthians 13:4-8a NLT * 1 John 3:18 NKJV * 1 John 4:18 NKJV * 1 John 4:21 NKJV

DAY

19 ....

You are made perfect in love.

_____
_____
_____
_____
_____
_____
_____
_____
_____
_____
_____
_____
_____
_____
_____
_____
_____
_____
_____
_____
_____
_____

Brethren, if a man is overtaken in any trespass, you who are spiritual restore such a one in a spirit of gentleness, considering yourself lest you also be tempted. Bear one another's burdens, and so fulfill the law of Christ. * For you, brethren have been called to liberty; only do not use liberty as an opportunity for the flesh, but through love serve one another. For all the law is fulfilled in one word, even in this: "You shall love your neighbor as yourself." * Therefore, as we have opportunity, let us do good to all, especially to those who are of the household of faith. * For by grace you have been saved through faith, and that not of yourselves; it is the gift of God, not of works, lest anyone should boast. For we are His workmanship, created in Christ Jesus for good works, which God prepared beforehand that we should walk in them. * I, therefore, the prisoner of the Lord, beseech you to walk worthy of the calling with which you were called, with all lowliness and gentleness, with longsuffering, bearing with one another in love, endeavoring to keep the unity of the Spirit in the bond of peace. * Having then gifts differing according to the grace that is given to us, let us use them: if prophecy, let us prophesy in proportion to our faith; or ministry, let us use it in our ministering; he who teaches, in teaching; he who exhorts, in exhortation; he who gives, with liberality; he who leads, with diligence; he who shows mercy, with cheerfulness. * Amen and Amen.

Galatians 6:1-2 NKJV * Galatians 5:13-14 NKJV * Galatians 5:10 NKJV * Ephesians 2:8-10 NKJV * Ephesians 4:1-3 NKJV * Romans 12:6-8 NKJV * Psalm 41:13b NKJV

20.....................................

How is God calling you to serve one another?

_____

_____

_____

_____

_____

_____

_____

_____

_____

_____

_____

_____

_____

_____

_____

_____

_____

_____

_____

_____

_____

_____

DAY 21

The effective fervent prayer of a righteous man
avails much. * The righteous keep moving
forward and those with clean hands become
stronger and stronger. * Indeed we count them
blessed who endure. You have heard of the
perseverance of Job and seen the end intended by
the Lord — that the Lord is very compassionate
and merciful. * Therefore we also, since we are
surrounded by so great a cloud of witnesses, let
us lay aside every weight, and the sin which so
easily ensnares us, and let us run with endurance
the race that is set before us, looking unto Jesus,
the author and finisher of our faith, who for the
joy that was set before Him endured the cross,
despising the shame, and has sat down at the
right hand of the throne of God. * Now to Him
who is able to keep you from stumbling, and to
present you faultless before the presence of His
glory with exceeding joy, to God our Savior, who
alone is wise, be glory and majesty, dominion and
power, both now and forever. Amen.

James 5:16b NKJV * Job 17:9 NLT * James 5:11
NKJV * Hebrews 12:1-2 NKJV * Jude 24-25 NKJV

DAY

21 ....

Focus on Jesus!

_____
_____
_____
_____
_____
_____
_____
_____
_____
_____
_____
_____
_____
_____
_____
_____
_____
_____
_____
_____
_____
_____

Worship God. * Holy, holy, holy, Lord God Almighty, Who was and is and is to come! * You are worthy, O Lord, to receive glory and honor and power; for You created all things, and by Your will they exist and were created. * You are worthy to take the scroll, and to open its seals; for You were slain, and have redeemed us to God by Your blood. Out of every tribe and tongue and people and nation, and have made us kings and priests to our God; and we shall reign on the earth. * Worthy is the Lamb who was slain to receive power and riches and wisdom, and strength and honor and glory and blessing! * Blessing and honor and glory and power be to Him who sits on the throne, and to the Lamb, forever and ever! * We give You thanks, O Lord God Almighty, the One who is and who was and who is to come, because You have taken Your great power and reigned. The nations were angry, and Your wrath has come, and the time of the dead, that they should be judged, and that You should reward Your servants the prophets and the saints, and those who fear Your name, small and great, and should destroy those who destroy the earth. * The grace of our Lord Jesus Christ be with you all. Amen.

Revelation 22:9b NKJV * Revelation 4:8b NKJV *
Revelation 4:11 NKJV * Revelation 5:9-10 NKJV *
Revelation 5:12 NKJV * Revelation 5:13b *
Revelation 11:17-18 NKJV * Revelation 22:21
NKJV

DAY

22 . . . .

Worship God.

_____
_____
_____
_____
_____
_____
_____
_____
_____
_____
_____
_____
_____
_____
_____
_____
_____
_____
_____
_____
_____
_____
_____

DAY 23

The first time I was brought before the judge, no
one was with me. Everyone had abandoned me. I
hope it will not be counted against them. But the
Lord stood with me and gave me strength, that I
might preach the Good News in all its fullness for
all the Gentiles to hear. And he saved me from
certain death. * I pray that from his glorious
unlimited resources he will give you mighty inner
strength through his Holy Spirit. * And may you
have the power to understand, as all God's people
should, how wide, how long, how high, and how
deep his love really is. May you experience the
love of Christ, though it is so great you will never
fully understand it. Then you will be filled with
the fullness of life and power that comes from
God. * We also pray that you will be strengthened
with his glorious power so that you will have all
the patience and endurance you need. May you
be filled with joy, always thanking the Father,
who has enabled you to share the inheritance that
belongs to God's holy people, who live in the
light. For he has rescued us from the one who
rules in the kingdom of darkness, and he has
brought us into the Kingdom of his dear Son. *
Yes, and the Lord will deliver me from every evil
attack and will bring me safely to his heavenly

Kingdom. To God be the glory forever and ever.
Amen.

2 Timothy 2:16-17 NLT * Ephesians 3:16 NLT *
Ephesians 3:18-19 NLT * Colossians 1:11-13 NLT *
2 Timothy 2:18 NLT

DAY

23 . . . .

The Lord will stand with you and give you strength.

_____

_____

_____

_____

_____

_____

_____

_____

_____

_____

_____

_____

_____

_____

_____

_____

_____

_____

_____

_____

DAY 24

God has purchased our freedom with his blood and has forgiven all our sins. * So if the Son sets you free, you will indeed be free. * And you will know the truth, and the truth will set you free. * This truth gives them the confidence of eternal life, which God promised them before the world began — and he cannot lie. * But people who aren't Christians can't understand these truths of God's Spirit. It all sounds foolish to them because only those who have the Spirit can understand what the Spirit means. * So now there is no condemnation for those who belong to Christ. For the power of the life-giving Spirit has freed you through Christ Jesus from the power of sin that leads to death. * So Christ has really set us free. Now make sure that you stay free, and don't get tied up again in slavery to the law. * My dear brothers and sisters, may the grace of our Lord Jesus Christ be with you all. Amen.

Colossians 1:14 NLT * John 8: 36 NLT * John 8:32 NLT * Titus 1:2 NLT * 1 Corinthians 2:14 NLT * Romans 8:1-2 NLT * Galatians 5:1 NLT * Galatians 6:18 NLT

DAY

24..................................

The truth sets you free.

_____

_____

_____

_____

_____

_____

_____

_____

_____

_____

_____

_____

_____

_____

_____

_____

_____

_____

_____

_____

DAY 25

When I thought how to understand this, it was too painful for me—until I went into the sanctuary of God; then I understood their end. * O house of Jacob, come and let us walk in the light of the LORD. * For you were once in darkness, but now you are light in the Lord. Walk as children of light (for the fruit of the Spirit is in all goodness, righteousness, and truth), finding out what is acceptable to the Lord. * Therefore be imitators of God as dear children. And walk in love, as Christ also has loved us and given Himself for us, an offering and a sacrifice to God for a sweet-smelling aroma. * As you therefore have received Christ Jesus the Lord, so walk in Him, rooted and built up in Him and established in the faith as you have been taught, abounding in it with thanksgiving. * And though the Lord gives you the bread of adversity and the water of affliction, yet your teachers will not be moved into a corner anymore, but your eyes shall see your teachers. Your ears shall hear a word behind you, saying, "This is the way, walk in it," whenever you turn to the right hand or whenever you turn to the left. * To God, alone wise, be glory through Jesus Christ forever. Amen.

Psalm 73:16-17 NKJV * Isaiah 2:5 NKJV *
Ephesians 5:8-10 NKJV * Ephesians 5:1-2 NKJV *
Colossians 2:6 NKJV * Isaiah 30:20-21 NKJV *
Romans 16:27 NKJV

25 . . . .

Bring every issue into the light of the Lord.

_____
_____
_____
_____
_____
_____
_____
_____
_____
_____
_____
_____
_____
_____
_____
_____
_____
_____
_____
_____
_____
_____
_____

DAY 26

God is not a man, that he should lie. He is not a human, that he should change his mind. Has he ever spoken and failed to act? Has he ever promised and not carried it through? * God is faithful, by whom you were called into the fellowship of His Son, Jesus Christ our Lord. * If we are faithless, He remains faithful; He cannot deny Himself. * Let us hold fast the confession of our hope without wavering, for He who promised is faithful. * No temptation has overtaken you except such as is common to man; but God is faithful, who will not allow you to be tempted beyond what you are able, but with the temptation will also make the way of escape, that you may be able to bear it. * To God, alone wise, be glory through Jesus Christ forever. Amen.

Numbers 23:19 NLT * 1 Corinthians 1:9 NKJV * 2 Timothy 2:13 NKJV * Hebrews 10:23 NKJV * 1 Corinthians 10:13 NKJV * Romans 16:27 NKJV

26 ....

He who promised is faithful.

_____

_____

_____

_____

_____

_____

_____

_____

_____

_____

_____

_____

_____

_____

_____

_____

_____

_____

_____

DAY 27

Seek the LORD while he may be found; call on him
while he is near. Let the wicked forsake their
ways and the unrighteous their thoughts. Let
them turn to the LORD, and he will have mercy on
them, and to our God, for he will freely pardon. *
Finally, brothers and sisters, whatever is true,
whatever is noble, whatever is right, whatever is
pure, whatever is lovely, whatever is admirable —
if anything is excellent or praiseworthy — think
about such things. * Keep this Book of the Law
always on your lips; meditate on it day and night,
so that you may be careful to do everything
written in it. Then you will be prosperous and
successful. * I have hidden your word in my heart
that I might not sin against you. * My love to all of
you in Christ Jesus. Amen.

Isaiah 55:6-7 NIV * Philippians 4:8 NIV * Joshua
1:8 NIV * Psalm 119:11 NIV * 1 Corinthians 16:24
NIV

DAY

27 ....

Right thinking leads to right actions.

_____
_____
_____
_____
_____
_____
_____
_____
_____
_____
_____
_____
_____
_____
_____
_____
_____
_____
_____
_____
_____
_____

DAY 28

They shall be mine, says the LORD of hosts, in the day when I make up my treasured possession, and I will spare them as a man spares his son who serves him. * As a father shows compassion to his children, so the LORD shows compassion to those who fear him. * For as high as the heavens are above the earth, so great is his steadfast love toward those who fear him. * But the steadfast love of the LORD is from everlasting to everlasting on those who fear him, and his righteousness to children's children, to those who keep his covenant and remember to do his commandments. * Then once more you shall see the distinction between the righteous and the wicked, between one who serves God and one who does not serve him. * For behold, the day is coming, burning like an oven, when all the arrogant and all evildoers will be stubble. The day that is coming shall set them ablaze, says the LORD of hosts, so that it will leave them neither root nor branch. But for you who fear my name, the sun of righteousness shall rise with healing in its wings. You shall go out leaping like calves from the stall. And you shall tread down the wicked, for they will be ashes under the soles of your feet, on the day when I act, says the LORD of hosts. * Amen and Amen!

Malachi 3:17 ESV * Psalm 103:13 ESV * Psalm 103:11ESV * Psalm 103:17-18 ESV * Malachi 3:18 ESV * Malachi 4:1-3 ESV * Psalm 72:19b ESV

DAY

28 . . . .

You are God's treasured possession.

_____

_____

_____

_____

_____

_____

_____

_____

_____

_____

_____

_____

_____

_____

_____

_____

_____

_____

_____

_____

_____

_____

Surely goodness and mercy shall follow me all the days of my life; and I will dwell in the house of the LORD forever. * Blessed be the God and Father of our Lord Jesus Christ, who has blessed us with every spiritual blessing in the heavenly places in Christ, just as He chose us in Him before the foundation of the world, that we should be holy and without blame before Him in love, having predestined us to adoption as sons by Jesus Christ to Himself, according to the good pleasure of His will, to the praise of the glory of His grace, by which He made us accepted in the Beloved. In Him we have redemption through His blood, the forgiveness of sins, according to the riches of His grace which He made to abound toward us in all wisdom and prudence, having made known to us the mystery of His will, according to His good pleasure which He purposed in Himself. * Those who are planted in the house of the LORD shall flourish in the courts of our God. They shall still bear fruit in old age; they shall be fresh and flourishing, to declare that the LORD is upright; He is my rock, and there is no unrighteousness in Him. * Now to Him who is able to do exceedingly abundantly above all that we ask or think, according to the power that works in us, to Him be glory in the church by Christ Jesus to all generations, forever and ever. Amen.

Psalm 23:6 NKJV * Ephesians 1:3-9 NKJV * Psalm 92:13-15 NKJV * Ephesians 3:20-21 NKJV

29 . . . .

**One who flourishes has a close continual walk
with God.**

_____

_____

_____

_____

_____

_____

_____

_____

_____

_____

_____

_____

_____

_____

_____

_____

_____

_____

_____

_____

DAY 30

And not only that, but we also glory in tribulations, knowing that tribulation produces perseverance; and perseverance character; and character, hope. * Knowing God leads to self-control. Self-control leads to patient endurance, and patient endurance leads to godliness. Godliness leads to love for other Christians, and finally you will grow to have genuine love for everyone. The more you grow like this, the more you will become productive and useful in your knowledge of our Lord Jesus Christ. * For our present troubles are quite small and won't last very long. Yet they produce in us an immeasurably great glory that will last forever! * We are pressed on every side by troubles, but we are not crushed and broken. We are perplexed, but we don't give up and quit. We are hunted down but God never abandons us. We get knocked down, but we get up again and keep going. * So we don't look at the troubles we can see right now; rather, we look forward to what we have not yet seen. For the troubles we see will soon be over, but the joys to come will last forever. * This hope we have as an anchor of the soul, both sure and steadfast, and which enters the Presence behind the veil. * Grace be with you all. Amen.

Romans 5:3-4 NKJV * 2 Peter 1:6-8 NLT * 2
Corinthians 4:17 NLT * 2 Corinthians 4:8-9 NLT *
2 Corinthians 4:18 NLT * Hebrews 6:19 NKJV *
Hebrews 13:25 NKJV

DAY

30 . . . .

Why does knowing God lead to self-control?

_____

_____

_____

_____

_____

_____

_____

_____

_____

_____

_____

_____

_____

_____

_____

_____

_____

_____

_____

_____

_____

_____

DAY 31

Righteousness guards him whose way is blameless, but wickedness overthrows the sinner. * For whatever is born of God overcomes the world. And this is the victory that has overcome the world—our faith. Who is he who overcomes the world, but he who believes that Jesus is the Son of God? * You are of God, little children, and have overcome them, because He who is in you is greater than he who is in the world. * These things I have spoken to you, that in Me you may have peace. In the world you will have tribulations; but be of good cheer, I have overcome the world. * Peace I leave with you, My peace I give to you; not as the world gives do I give to you. Let not your heart be troubled, neither let it be afraid. * But thanks be to God, who gives us victory through our Lord Jesus Christ. * To God our Savior, who alone is wise, be glory and majesty, dominion and power, both now and forever. Amen.

Proverbs 13:6 NKJV * 1 John 5:4-5 NKJV * 1 John 4:4 NKJV * John 16:33 NKJV * John 14:27 NKJV * 1 Corinthians 15:57 NKJV * Jude 1:25 NKJV

DAY

31 ....

With Jesus Christ as your Savior, you will overcome.

_____
_____
_____
_____
_____
_____
_____
_____
_____
_____
_____
_____
_____
_____
_____
_____
_____
_____
_____
_____
_____
_____
_____
_____

DAY 32

God is in the midst of her, she shall not be moved; God shall help her, just at the break of dawn. * "No weapon formed against you shall prosper, and every tongue which rises against you in judgment You shall condemn. This is the heritage of the servants of the LORD, and their righteousness is from Me," says the LORD. * You are of God, little children, and have overcome them, because He who is in you is greater than he who is in the world. * Do not marvel my brethren, if the world hates you. * If the world hates you, you know that it hated Me before it hated you. * He who hates Me hates My Father also. * If we receive the witness of men, the witness of God is greater; for this is the witness of God which He has testified of His Son. He who believes in the Son of God has the witness in himself; he who does not believe God has made Him a liar, because he has not believed the testimony that God has given of His Son. And this is the testimony: that God has given us eternal life, and this life is in His Son. He who has the Son has life; he who does not have the Son of God does not have life. * And Jesus said to them, "I am the bread of life. He who comes to Me shall never hunger, and he who believes in Me shall never thirst. * Most assuredly, I say to you, he who believes in Me has everlasting life. I am the bread of life. * Now to Him who is able to keep you from stumbling, and to present you faultless before the presence of His glory with exceeding joy, to God our Savior, who alone is wise, be glory and majesty, dominion and power, both now and forever. Amen.

Psalm 46:5 NKJV * Isaiah 54:17 NKJV * 1 John 4:4 NKJV * 1 John 3:13 NKJV * John 15:18 NKJV * John 15:23 NKJV * 1 John 5:9-12 NKJV * John 6:35 NKJV * John 6:47-48 NKJV * Jude 1:24-25 NKJV

DAY

32 ....

The world's hatred is weak in comparison to God's love.

_____

_____

_____

_____

_____

_____

_____

_____

_____

_____

_____

_____

_____

_____

_____

_____

_____

_____

_____

But the Lord is faithful who will establish you and guard you from the evil one. * The LORD is your keeper; the LORD is your shade at your right hand. The sun shall not strike you by day, nor the moon by night. The LORD shall preserve you from all evil; He shall preserve your soul. The LORD shall preserve your going out and your coming in from this time forth, and even forevermore. * Now may the God of peace Himself sanctify you completely; and may your whole spirit, soul, and body be preserved blameless at the coming of our Lord Jesus Christ. He who calls you is faithful, who also will do it. * Therefore let him who thinks he stands take heed lest he fall. No temptation has overtaken you except such as is common to man; but God is faithful, who will not allow you to be tempted beyond what you are able, but with the temptation will also make the way of escape, that you may be able to bear it. * Awake, you who sleep, arise from the dead, and Christ will give you light. * Grace be with all those who love our Lord Jesus Christ in sincerity. Amen.

2 Thessalonians 3:3 NKJV * Psalm 121:5-8 NKJV * 1 Thessalonians 5:23-24 NKJV * 1 Corinthians 10:12-13 NKJV * Ephesians 5:14 NKJV * Ephesians 6:24 NKJV

DAY

33 ....

The Lord will establish you.

_____

_____

_____

_____

_____

_____

_____

_____

_____

_____

_____

_____

_____

_____

_____

_____

_____

_____

_____

_____

DAY 34

When I think of the wisdom and scope of God's plan, I fall to my knees and pray to the Father, the Creator of everything in heaven and on earth. I pray that from his glorious, unlimited resources he will give you mighty inner strength through His Holy Spirit. And I pray that Christ will be more and more at home in your hearts as you trust in him. May your roots go down deep into the soil of God's marvelous love. And may you have the power to understand, as all God's people should, how wide, how long, how high, and how deep his love really is. * We know how much God loves us, and we have put our trust in him. God is love and all who live in love live in God, and God lives in them. And as we live in God, our love grows more perfect. So we will not be afraid on the day of judgment, but we can face him with confidence because we are like Christ here in this world. Such love has no fear because perfect love expels all fear. If we are afraid, it is for fear of judgment, and this shows that his love has not been perfected in us. We love each other as a result of his loving us first. * May God's grace be upon all who love our Lord Jesus Christ with an undying love. * Amen and Amen.

Ephesians 3:14-19 NLT * 1 John 4:16-19 NLT *
Ephesians 6:24 NLT * Psalm 72:19b NLT

DAY

34 ....

Do you grasp how deep God's love is for you?

_____

_____

_____

_____

_____

_____

_____

_____

_____

_____

_____

_____

_____

_____

_____

_____

_____

_____

_____

_____

_____

DAY 35

Victory comes from you, O LORD, may your blessings rest on your people. * Listen to my cry for help, my King and my God, for I will never pray to anyone but you. Listen to my voice in the morning, LORD, each morning I bring my requests to you and wait expectantly. * I cried out to the LORD, and he answered me from his holy mountain. I lay down and slept. I woke up in safety, for the LORD was watching over me. I am not afraid of ten thousand enemies who surround me on every side. Arise, O LORD! Rescue me, my God! Slap all my enemies in the face! Shatter the teeth of the wicked! * O God, you take no pleasure in wickedness; you cannot tolerate the slightest sin. Therefore, the proud will not be allowed to stand in your presence, for you hate all who do evil. You will destroy those who tell lies. The LORD detests murderers and deceivers. Because of your unfailing love, I can enter your house; with deepest awe I will worship at your Temple. Lead me in the right path, O LORD, or my enemies will conquer me. Tell me clearly what to do, and show me which way to turn. * Amen and Amen.

Psalm 3:8 NLT * Psalm 5:2-3 NLT * Psalm 3:4-7 NLT * Psalm 5:5-8 NLT * Psalm 72:19b NLT

DAY

35 ....

Pray expectantly.

_____
_____
_____
_____
_____
_____
_____
_____
_____
_____
_____
_____
_____
_____
_____
_____
_____
_____
_____
_____
_____
_____

DAY 36

The LORD is my light and my salvation; whom shall I fear? The LORD is the strength of my life; of whom shall I be afraid? * I would have lost heart, unless I had believed that I would see the goodness of the LORD in the land of the living. Wait on the LORD; be of good courage, and He shall strengthen your heart; wait, I say, on the LORD! * The LORD will give strength to His people; the LORD will bless His people with peace. * Blessed be the LORD, because He has heard the voice of my supplications! The LORD is my strength and my shield; my heart trusted in Him, and I am helped; therefore my heart greatly rejoices, and with my song I will praise Him. The Lord is their strength, And He is the saving refuge of His anointed. Save Your people, and bless Your inheritance; shepherd them also, and bear them up forever. * Blessed be the LORD forevermore! Amen and Amen.

Psalm 27:1 NKJV * Psalm 27:13-14 NKJV * Psalm 29:11 NKJV * Psalm 28:6-9 NKJV * Psalm 89:52 NKJV

36 ....

I would have lost heart, unless I had believed that I would see the goodness of the LORD in the land of the living.

_____

_____

_____

_____

_____

_____

_____

_____

_____

_____

_____

_____

_____

_____

_____

_____

_____

_____

_____

DAY 37

O LORD my God, you have done many miracles
for us. Your plans for us are too numerous to list.
If I tried to recite all your wonderful deeds, I
would never come to the end of them. * Who else
among the gods is like you, O LORD? Who is
glorious in holiness like you — so awesome in
splendor, performing such wonders? You raised
up your hand, and the earth swallowed our
enemies. With unfailing love you will lead this
people whom you have ransomed. You will guide
them in your strength to the place where your
holiness dwells. * "My thoughts are completely
different from yours," says the LORD. "And my
ways are far beyond anything you could imagine.
For just as the heavens are higher than the earth,
so are my ways higher than your ways and my
thoughts higher than your thoughts. * "Be just
and fair to all," says the LORD. "Do what is right
and good, for I am coming soon to rescue you.
Blessed are those who are careful to do this.
Blessed are those who honor my Sabbath days of
rest by refusing to work. And blessed are those
who keep themselves from doing wrong." * I will
bring them also to my holy mountain of Jerusalem
and will fill them with joy in my house of prayer.
I will accept their burnt offerings and sacrifices,
because my Temple will be called a house of

prayer for all nations. For the Sovereign LORD, who brings back the outcasts of Israel, says: I will bring others, too, besides my people Israel. * I will praise your mighty deeds, O Sovereign LORD. I will tell everyone that you alone are just and good. * We will not hide these truths from our children, but will tell the next generation about the glorious deeds of the LORD. We will tell of his power and the mighty miracles he did. * So the next generation might know them—even the children not yet born—so they in turn might teach their children. So each generation can set its hope anew on God, remembering his glorious miracles and obeying his commands. * Now to Him who is able to do exceedingly abundantly above all that we ask or think, according to the power that works in us, to Him be glory in the church by Christ Jesus to all generations, forever and ever. Amen.

Psalm 40:5 NLT * Exodus 15:11-13 NLT * Isaiah 55:8-9 NLT * Isaiah 56:1-2 NLT * Isaiah 56:7-8 NLT * Psalm 71:16 NLT * Psalm 78:4 NLT * Psalm 78:6-7 NLT * Ephesians 3:20-21 NKJV

DAY

37 ....

God is able to do exceedingly abundantly above
all you ask or think, and He wants to.

_____
_____
_____
_____
_____
_____
_____
_____
_____
_____
_____
_____
_____
_____
_____
_____
_____
_____
_____
_____
_____

DAY 38

Blessed are those who mourn, for they shall be comforted. * Also He spoke this parable to some who trusted in themselves that they were righteous, and despised others: "Two men went up to the temple to pray, one a Pharisee and the other a tax collector. The Pharisee stood and prayed thus with himself, 'God, I thank You that I am not like other men — extortioners, unjust, adulterers, or even as this tax collector. I fast twice a week; I give tithes of all that I possess.' And the tax collector, standing afar off, would not so much as raise his eyes to heaven, but beat his breast, saying, 'God, be merciful to me a sinner!' I tell you, this man went down to his house justified rather than the other; for everyone who exalts himself will be humbled, and he who humbles himself will be exalted." * For all have sinned; all fall short of God's glorious standard. Yet now God in his gracious kindness declares us not guilty. He has done this through Christ Jesus, who has freed us by taking away our sins. For God sent Jesus to take the punishment for our sins and to satisfy God's anger against us. We are made right with God when we believe that Jesus shed his blood, sacrificing his life for us. God was being entirely fair and just when he did not punish those who sinned in former times. And he is entirely fair and just in this present time when he declares sinners to be right in his sight because they believe in Jesus. Can we boast, then, that we have done anything to be accepted by God? No, because our acquittal is not based on our good deeds. It is based on our faith. So we are made right with God through faith and not by obeying the law. * To God, alone wise, be glory through Jesus Christ forever. Amen.

Matthew 5:4 NKJV * Luke 18:9-14 NKJV * Romans 3:23-28 NLT * Romans 16:27 NKJV

38 . . . .

Are you quick to ask God to forgive you of your sin?

_____

_____

_____

_____

_____

_____

_____

_____

_____

_____

_____

_____

_____

_____

_____

_____

_____

_____

_____

_____

_____

DAY 39

I thank my God upon every remembrance of you, always in every prayer of mine making request for you all with joy. * That the God of our Lord Jesus Christ, the Father of glory, may give to you the spirit of wisdom and revelation in the knowledge of Him, the eyes of your understanding being enlightened; that you may know what is the hope of His calling, what are the riches of the glory of His inheritance in the saints and what is the exceeding greatness of His power toward us who believe, according to the working of His mighty power which He worked in Christ when He raised Him from the dead and seated Him at His right hand in the heavenly places, far above all principality and power and might and dominion, and every name that is named, not only in this age but also in that which is to come. * For this reason we also, since the day we heard it, do not cease to pray for you, and to ask that you may be filled with the knowledge of His will in all wisdom and spiritual understanding, that you may walk worthy of the Lord, fully pleasing Him, being fruitful in every good work and increasing in the knowledge of God; strengthened with all might, according to His glorious power, for all patience and longsuffering with joy; giving thanks to the Father who has qualified us to be partakers of the inheritance of the saints in the light. * That Christ may dwell in your hearts through faith: that you, being rooted and grounded in love, may be able to comprehend with all the saints what is the width and length and depth and height—to know the love of Christ which passes knowledge; that you may be filled with all the fullness of God. * He has delivered us from the power of darkness and conveyed us into the kingdom of the Son of His love, in whom we have redemption through His blood, the forgiveness of sins. * All who are with me greet you. Greet those who love us in the faith. Grace be with you all. Amen.

Philippians 1:3-4 NKJV * Ephesians 1:17-21 NKJV * Colossians 1:9-12 NKJV * Ephesians 3:17-19 NKJV * Colossians 1:13-14 NKJV * Titus 3:15 NKJV

DAY

39 ....

Pray for the church.
Revival of the hearts.

_____
_____
_____
_____
_____
_____
_____
_____
_____
_____
_____
_____
_____
_____
_____
_____
_____
_____
_____
_____

DAY 40

Trust in the LORD, and do good; dwell in the land and befriend faithfulness. * Trust in the LORD with all your heart, and do not lean on your own understanding. In all your ways acknowledge him, and he will make straight your paths. Be not wise in your own eyes; fear the LORD, and turn away from evil. It will be healing to your flesh and refreshment to your bones. * Trust in the LORD forever, for the LORD GOD is an everlasting rock. * Trust in him at all times, O people; pour out your heart before him; God is a refuge for us. * Delight yourself in the LORD, and he will give you the desires of your heart. * But seek first the kingdom of God and his righteousness, and all these things will be added to you. * Rejoice in the Lord always; again I will say, Rejoice. * Commit your way to the LORD; trust in him, and he will act. * Commit your work to the LORD, and your plans will be established. * My love be with you all in Christ Jesus. Amen.

Psalm 37:3 ESV * Proverbs 3:5-8 ESV * Isaiah 26:4 ESV * Psalm 62:8 ESV * Psalm 37:4 ESV * Matthew 6:33 ESV * Philippians 4:4 ESV * Psalm 37:5 ESV * Proverbs 16:3 ESV * 1 Corinthians 16:24 ESV

DAY

40 ....

**Trust in the Lord forever.
May He guide your every endeavor.**

_____
_____
_____
_____
_____
_____
_____
_____
_____
_____
_____
_____
_____
_____
_____
_____
_____
_____
_____
_____
_____

AUTHOR

....

Alysa VanderWeerd is also the author of the poetry book, *Life.*, and the 365- day devotional, *Mountaintop Mornings*. Her *In His Presence* bible study curriculum series includes: *the End: The Book of Revelation*, *Redeeming The Time: Psalm 16:11* and *Radical Living: The Book of James.*

She has her Bachelors in History with a minor in English from the University of California- Irvine. She has her Master of Arts in History from the University of California- Riverside; and is currently working on her Doctorate in Education in Community Care and Counseling: Family and Marriage from Liberty University.

For more about Alysa, visit relentlessprayer.org.

Made in the USA
Columbia, SC
02 March 2020

88588069R00065